C000134981

'I first encountered Glyn
coming across evangelists
comfortable in their own
Jones and The Light Project.

'This is book is fresh bread. Engaging story telling by a
man who "does what Jesus says", who prays and sees the
extraordinary in ordinary situations, who lives his faith,
not just explains it, Honest, vulnerable, engaging. Loved
it!'
Rev Dr Jill Duff, Bishop of Lancaster

'This is a wonderful book and I couldn't wait for the next
story, as each one has a delight and beauty all its own.
Glyn is real and funny, and yet all these encounters come
from a deep, deep trust in the God who is out there and
who loves us. This is an infectious book and I am hoping
to catch what Glyn has got, and I hope you do too.'
Keith Sinclair, Bishop of Birkenhead

'Glyn uses his wide experience of doing evangelism to
engage us with a variety of stories. They are worth
considering and then informing our activities.'
*Revd Canon Dave Male, Head of Evangelism and Discipleship,
Archbishop's Council, Church of England*

THE PEG AND THE PUMICE STONE

And other true stories to develop good news habits

Glyn Jones

instant
apostle

First published in Great Britain in 2019

Instant Apostle

The Barn
1 Watford House Lane
Watford
Herts
WD17 1BJ

Every effort has been made to seek permission to use copyright material reproduced in this book. The publisher apologises for those cases where permission might not have been sought and, if notified, will formally seek permission at the earliest opportunity.

The views and opinions expressed in this work are those of the author and do not necessarily reflect the views and opinions of the publisher.

British Library Cataloguing-in-Publication Data

A catalogue record for this book is available from the British Library.

This book and all other Instant Apostle books are available from Instant Apostle:

Website: www.instantapostle.com
E-mail: info@instantapostle.com

ISBN 978-1-912726-00-4

Printed in Great Britain.

Thanks to my wife Raphaëlle and my two daughters, Betty and Cerys – for helping me keep it real.

To everyone at The Light Project who has taught me so much about following Jesus.

Contents

Foreword

'We met under a cherry tree in France twelve years ago. The sun was blazing and we enjoyed its shade as we spoke about evangelism, the idea of working together in Chester and our love for Jesus. My life has never been the same since. Nor has the life of The Light Project.

'Being a friend of Glyn's has enthused the adventure that I'm on of seeking to follow in the slipstream of Jesus. So much of what I do as an evangelist is because I am deeply encouraged by Glyn, who naturally oozes good news and shows me time and time again the joy of sharing the best news that this world has been graced with.

'Glyn is the most exuberant evangelist I know. His love for people and warm engagement with everyone he meets encourages me to do likewise. I now ask everyone who serves me at coffee shops, petrol stations, cashiers or anyone I randomly meet, 'How is your day going?' It's so simple. But the care and genuine compassion I see in how Glyn engages with people is truly infectious. This book flows from the real deal. Glyn really does tell others about Jesus wherever he goes!

'I first read *The Peg and the Pumice Stone* on a train. It was jam packed. There were plenty of snorts and laugh-out-loud moments as I devoured the stories. I could handle the looks and raised eyebrows as I guffawed, but when a tear or two fell down my cheek and I sniffled over some of the heartbreaking stories I felt I needed to engage with those around me about what I was reading and in a small way to reassure them that I was alright!

'The lady sitting next to me was fascinated with Glyn's story and proceeded to pour out her heart for more than an hour about her family and those she had lost. I only wished that I had a hard copy of Glyn's book with me at the time, as this really is the kind of book that I want to give away to people I meet! The stories are uplifting, faith affirming and will help you share your faith naturally with those you meet. The next best thing to hanging out with Glyn and observing his infectious Jesus sharing is to read his book.

'Lastly, Glyn and I, alongside our co-leader Gaz, head up The Light Project College and Collective. How about training with us in how to demonstrate the gospel? We offer a degree in partnership with the University of Chester in Theology, Mission and Evangelism and are always looking to train up pioneers who will go and make countless disciples!'

Rev Chris Duffett, Baptist Evangelist and President of the Baptist Union of Great Britain (2011–2012)

1

A Broken Candle

It is better to do something with what you don't have, than to do nothing with what you do have.

I was driving home. It was early November and it had been a glorious sunny day. It was that time of year when you make the most of those good days, and I pulled over to snatch a stroll in the park before the last of the sunlight faded. I felt grateful that day; grateful for my family, my kids, my friends and my job. I had nearly lost it all ten years earlier, until an unexpected hope burst into my life. This hope had changed everything for me. Acutely aware of my good fortune, I gazed across the empty park, brimming with gratitude.

I sat down on a bench. I felt an urge to kneel down and say thank you to God for everything, but felt awkward even though no one else was around. What if someone saw me? I overcame my nagging pride and knelt down on the ground. I leaned on the bench and gently closed my eyes. As I thanked God, I heard the birds arguing on the branches and the leaves rustling in the trees, announcing the arrival of wetter and windier weather. As I prayed, an unexpected sound interrupted the moment – it was the sound of gravel underfoot. Someone was approaching. I began to picture the scene of me kneeling on the ground and realised how odd this might look to a passer-by. I panicked.

It was too late to stand, and I experienced that momentary irritation when someone spoils an especially good moment. It was a big park; why couldn't they walk somewhere else? Why did they have to walk past *me* and interrupt *my* moment? I weighed up the options – I could pretend to be looking for my keys to make this look slightly less weird, or just keep my head down and hope for the best. I figured most people would be too embarrassed to interrupt and so I froze with my head down and eyes tightly closed. The footsteps approached – crunch, crunch, crunch – and then continued past me in a regular fashion, without pausing. They petered out into the distance, leaving me alone with the sounds of birds.

I peered out of one eye – all clear. I stood up, stretched my stiff knees and walked on with slight relief. As I strolled towards the car, I spied in the distance the gravel-cruncher ahead of me and instinctively dawdled – no need to hurry now, was there? However, as I slowed, he too seemed to be moving at a snail's pace and the distance between us diminished with each step.

I loitered even more, but despite a sterling effort, I began to gain on my companion. He was a tall man, wearing a dark jacket with the collar turned up. His shoulders were hunched and his hands were tucked tightly into the coat pockets. The north wind was not far away. There was nothing for it; I was going to have to make a dash past him and pretend that a man kneeling at a bench, praying, was a normal thing in these parts. I accelerated.

As my pace quickened, something deep inside me groaned for this man. It formed as a whisper in my heart: 'Give him what you have.'

I know this whisper and I know the thought process that follows, all too well. It starts with me considering that God may be speaking to me and finishes with me proposing logical and rational reasons why this course of action would not be feasible or appropriate. I then propose another alternative, to appease any sense of my unease or guilt. God and I are well rehearsed in such routines, much, I am sure, to the frustration and amusement of the Almighty. 'Give him what you have' – honestly!

I checked my bag, and except for a broken candle and some crumpled papers, I had nothing meaningful. No money, no Bible and nothing remotely spiritual. Only my car keys and he certainly wasn't getting those. No, I had nothing to give this man. I mentally explained to God why I wouldn't be able to help him out on this occasion and even started to hum to myself to drown out any other unreasonable suggestions from the Supreme Being. 'Give him what you have' – the words stirred in my heart with gravity.

I was only yards behind the man, but the sense was so urgent now that I looked again in my bag. I rooted underneath the broken candle. The reason I was carrying a broken candle is not entirely without interest. I had spent the previous day taking photographs of people holding unlit candles – they were to be used in an exhibition entitled 'You are the light of the world'. People have the potential, like a candle, to emit light and warmth – once lit by God. However, this candle had broken and it didn't seem fitting to photograph someone as a broken candle, so it had been consigned to my bag.

I toyed with the candle as I passed the dawdler, and rehearsed my lines: 'Hello, I'm the weirdo who was kneeling down in front of the bench back there. Just in case you thought that wasn't weird enough, here is a broken candle as a gift.' No, no, no, far too weird!

I cleared my throat and took another tack.

'Erm, would you happen to know if there is a bonfire being held in the park this year?' I asked, in a casual kind of way. My voice came out two octaves too high. I dragged it down and kicked some gravel in a more masculine way.

'No,' came the indifferent reply. There was an unimpressed look in his eye of 'Weren't you that weirdo back there?'

Now I could see him face to face. He was a broad fellow with a donkey jacket, tidy stubble, and a look on his face that said, 'I've no time for fools.'

'Listen, I have something for you,' I said, with all the seriousness I could muster, and looked squarely at his feet. I stretched out my arm and held out the broken candle as it drooped over the side of my hand. I looked up slowly to gauge the response.

He looked at it, and looked at me, and then back at the candle. 'Why you are giving me a broken candle?' he said, blankly. A fair question.

'It's hope,' I blurted out. 'Yes, hope.' I repeated it as if that would make it normal.

He looked at me, expressionless.

'Look,' I explained. 'I've been walking in the park this afternoon with an overwhelming sense of gratefulness – grateful for all that's good in my life, grateful for something that happened to me nearly ten years ago that changed my life. It gave me hope at a time of despair, and I wanted to give you some of that hope – this candle represents hope.'

Silence. He pondered.

And then I saw a change in his eye, a glimpse of his heart. A tear formed and then tears in both eyes. The big guy now looked at my feet. And then he did something I never expected. He leaned forward and put two big arms around me and held me. I felt like a little boy in his dad's arms. After what seemed a lifetime, he let go and dried his eyes. I said nothing.

He began to talk. He told me how Novembers loom for him with a sense of foreboding. How he had lost a family member years back in November in tragic circumstances and how every November a cloud settles over him and he dreads the month to come – it was 4th November, the eve of Bonfire night.

With growing animation, he explained, 'I am walking through this park, wondering how I will make it through November this year, and you walk up and give me this, and tell me it is hope.' He looked almost ecstatic.

I felt sad, humbled, and stupid for doubting God.

We walked on a little as dusk advanced and sat together on a log. We talked about his life and his loss. I told him about Jesus, who has a hope for us all. He had a pen and I went to write my number on the paper in my bag and found John's Gospel in the back pocket – odd I hadn't seen that before – so I gave it to him.

He took it, and I said a prayer for him. We shook hands and parted ways.

So often we think that we lack what we need to bring good news to people. We will be able to do it when we have more training, when we get the new minister, when we have the new materials, or the new youth worker, when the church roof is fixed, and so on. It becomes a well-oiled excuse for why we can't share the hope we have. It never seemed to stop Jesus.

Jesus had an uncanny ability to use the everyday things that surrounded Him – He gave thanks, blessed them and did the most extraordinary things. He took some mud from the ground and the blind man regained his sight, some loaves and fishes and hungry thousands ate plentifully, some ordinary fishermen and a Church was born. As my wife prays, let us see the extraordinary in the ordinary. It may be unorthodox, but it has a precedent.

We see Jesus, time and time again, doing remarkable things with everyday objects and not waiting for the resources He does not have. It is better to do something with what you don't have, than to do nothing with what you do have. As Madeleine Delbrêl says, 'We lack nothing essential. If we needed it, God would have already given it to us.'[1]

The problem arises when our faith lies in our resources and not in God. We should be grateful for all the things we have that are gifts from God, but when they become an excuse for inertia, we need reminding once again of the Giver and not the gift. This is a lesson that the Church comes back to every once in a while. We see it actioned in the lives of people such as St Francis of Assisi and Mother Teresa, who functioned with the bare essentials that God provided for them. Not all of us are called to live lives such as theirs, but we can practise the same principle of reliance and dependence on God. I'm going to call this the 'Bread and Fishes' principle of evangelism: look in your pocket, give thanks and bless whatever you find, be willing to ask God to use it – and expect the unexpected.

---

[1] A phrase from Madeleine Delbrêl, translated and paraphrased by Glyn Jones from Madeleine Delbrêl, *Oeuvres Complete*, Tomes VII, *La sainteté des gens ordinaires: Textes missionaires*, vol. 1. (Paris: Nouvelle Cité , 2009), pp23-24.

2

Car Boot Sale

Any church committed to making followers of Jesus will sooner or later have to deal with the likes of Boy Genius and the Virgin Mary – better start sooner rather than later, in my book.

Most years, with a group of friends or a local church, I run some kind of introduction to Christianity course: Alpha, Pilgrim, Christianity Explored, that sort of thing. I ask some of the students with whom I work to help me out, and often we tinker with it and tailor it to suit the people who have shown an interest in faith. I must admit, I love these times. In the patchwork of things I do, these are often the places where people take significant steps and where faith becomes theirs, personally. We have baptised many people following these courses – in churches, rivers and the sea – and they remain for me a key piece in the jigsaw puzzle of discipleship and evangelism.

However, while they remain an important part in people exploring faith, they can sometimes be quite heavy and intellectual in their content and, for some of my friends, they don't offer the right context. A while back, inspired by a TV documentary on Channel 4 called *Make Me a Christian*, we ran a course that involved not only examining the key ideas of Christianity, but also trying them out in practice. We got people to write prayers, try leading a church service, serve at a soup kitchen, take part in a prayer walk and, my personal favourite, design an evangelism event. All this, before any of them had signed on the dotted line of faith.

This particular year, we were joined by Boy Genius. I didn't know Boy Genius personally – he was the friend of a friend who thought that this might be a good place for him to field his questions. This guy was something else: Nietzsche, Aristotle, Plato, Socrates – he knew them all inside out. He could talk philosophy and religion like a Frenchman talks cheese. I suspect that he had polished off a few pastors and youth workers on his way to us, and his friend had probably sent him our way in desperation. In honesty, we all felt out of our depth and some of the discussion was, frankly, a little shallow for him. We skipped through the normal stuff and he single-handedly tossed around the topics like a circus juggler. As we met each week, it appeared that he was just nibbling and the subject matter was mere finger food.

While we couldn't match his IQ, he clearly enjoyed the time together and the friendships that developed. Reading Psalms at the summit of Snowdon and serving people in a soup kitchen clearly affected him. As a group, we began to bond, and a trust developed as the weeks went on. The last sessions were about grace. We discussed the concept over fried rice and argued about what it would look like today if we were all people of grace. And so the idea of the car boot sale was born. We all committed to playing our part and set the date to meet.

It was a cold, crisp Sunday morning, and one which promised to warm up gently as the day advanced. We met at 7am sharp and paid our £10 entry fee to the car boot sale. In terms of Sunday morning commitments, this group were showing great promise. We set our tarpaulin out amid the career car boot sellers and started to arrange our wares.

The week before at church, I had asked if anyone in the congregation would be willing to help us out by donating valuable objects to our car boot sale. I explained it was part of the course that I was running and gave my apologies for the following Sunday service, as I planned to be recovering in bed after an early start. Several people kindly pledged a variety of interesting objects including a painting, an iPod, and a pewter pot. These things, along with all the junk from my garage, were carefully placed on the tarpaulin in front of my car, surrounded by our bleary-eyed faith explorers.

We had agreed as a group together that if people wanted to buy something, we would sell it. But, if they wanted one of the donated items, they could only acquire it on one condition – that they received it as a free gift. They could give us nothing in return. If they wanted to know why, we would explain about the course we were doing and how we were trying to demonstrate the Christian concept of grace.

Soon people began to drift along and glance over the goods. We sold some bits and bobs; a book and some hand tools. Before long, a guy came over and asked about the painting. He was from Spain and we explained to him the deal. He seemed amused and pleased with the whole transaction, probably thinking what a strange bunch the British were. We told him about a guy at church who had painted it. It was the only painting he had ever done and it was a precious object for him. The Spanish guy loved the painting and was clearly moved by the gesture. He received it with great joy and gratitude and gave us a message for the artist. He was touched and so were we. Boy Genius seemed amused.

Shortly afterwards, a couple in their fifties meandered along and eyed up the pewter pot. 'How much for this?' they asked.

'How much is it worth to you?' we joked, clueless to the actual value of the object.

They looked at each other.

'I'll give you £20,' the man offered.

For a split second, I questioned why on earth I was a Christian and considered taking the money. Then Boy Genius piped up, 'You can have it.'

The guy paused, glanced at his wife, smiled and cautiously counted out £20.

'There you go,' he said, and handed Boy Genius the money.

Boy Genius didn't budge and his hands remained firmly in his pockets.

'You can have it,' he repeated.

The man paused again. He glanced at his wife and the look in her eyes indicated that she wanted it.

'OK, then.' He added £5 to his handful of notes and held them out.

'Sorry,' I interrupted. 'You can't have it for £25 – but you *can* take it for free, if you like.'

He tried pushing the money towards me, not amused.

I too, remained motionless.

'Sorry,' Boy Genius apologised. 'That's the condition – take it freely or don't take it at all.'

'You can't do that,' the man snapped.

He said it with such conviction that, for a split second, I wavered and nearly sold him the pot. Boy Genius didn't. He held his nerve and I could see that he was starting to enjoy this.

By this point, a small crowd had gathered to see what was going on – was a fight starting? Nothing like a little commotion to stir interest.

'I'm afraid we can,' Boy Genius insisted.

The guy's expression changed from indignation to almost hurt and he remonstrated with us.

People in the crowd egged him on, some to take it, some to up the offer.

Amid this little commotion, quietly and without a word, a young lady made her way through the milling crowd and drew close to the couple.

'Mum, Dad,' she said, gently, 'they are not going to give it to you. They don't want your money.'

The couple looked at us with an expression that suggested they felt genuinely robbed. With a note of resignation and bewilderment, they asked, 'Why?'

Boy Genius, who was not, and still is not, to my knowledge, a card-carrying Christian, stepped forward and addressed the crowd. With clarity, sensitivity and coherence, he explained to the whole group of gathered listeners what we were doing – everyone followed intently. A group of people standing silently naturally attracts others and, as he spoke, more people approached the stall. He explained that this was a picture of grace and how grace was crucial to what being a Christian means. The moment was priceless.

As he finished, people quietly began to confer with each other. I noticed the couple slowly withdrawing, leaving the pewter pot on the tarpaulin. Their daughter smiled apologetically at me and followed them. As the others began to drift away, a man who had been at the back of the crowd pushed his way forward. He had the wily face of a veteran car boot-seller. He picked up the pewter pot and turned it in his weathered hands. He looked it up and down, and with a cheeky little smile, he said, 'I'll have it.'

'Then it's yours,' we smiled back.

He grinned and walked away.

Boy Genius was thoughtful for the rest of the morning.

Now, I realise that you could raise valid objections to this approach to discipleship or evangelism, and you may be right. How can non-Christians present genuine faith authentically? What about sin and forgiveness and all the other bits about Jesus? Well, you are both right *and* wrong.

Faith is lived, not just explained. The reality is that Jesus Himself took a group of people who were willing to come with Him; I don't think the penny had dropped for most – if any – of them. What is more, not only did Jesus allow people to participate in His work, He also seemed quite comfortable with the notion of relying on them to complete His task. Jesus needed the guy with the boat to address the people on the shore, the woman to give Him a drink at the well, even the tax collectors to feed Him. You may argue that He didn't really need them, that He could have done a swift miracle or two to arrange things – but He didn't. He chose to involve and rely on broken people, to let them participate in His mission and His good news – just like He does with you and me.

I call this *Participative Evangelism*[2] and while I don't suggest it is the only way, I do think that it responds to a need many people have as they grapple to make sense of God. It's the need to work some things out in the doing of them, as well as trying to make sense of them in our heads. As a Church we often talk about *belong before you believe*,[3] but in my experience this often turns into *attend before you believe*. We assume that if people come to church on a Sunday morning then they will learn everything they

---

[2] A concept I have developed in my Master's thesis, *An Analysis and Critique of Evangelical Approaches to Evangelism in the 21st Century* (University of Chester, United Kingdom, 2012).
[3] A phrase first used by Grace Davie in her work *Religion in Britain Since 1945: Believing without Belonging* (Oxford: Blackwell, 1994).

need about being a follower of Jesus. The problem with pure attendance is that it soon becomes passive, and unless you take part and live it out, faith becomes an abstract idea. The good news was never given to people on a quest for clever ideas; it was given for those in desperate need of life.[4] So why not start out as you mean to go on? Let people see from the outset what this following Jesus entails – you never know, they might like it and it might teach us something in the process.

Participative Mission it is not without its challenges. At one of my live nativities in the centre of town with donkeys and hay bales, children were asking why the Virgin Mary looked so drawn and tired and had a cigarette falling out of the side of her mouth. In reality, *this* Virgin Mary was a recovering addict, on her fag break. She was also my friend, trying to fathom an enigmatic man called Jesus and what it meant to follow Him. Being part of that piece of evangelism was crucial for her, even if it may shock and baffle some of us.

This highlights another very real hurdle that we all should encounter as Church: the messiness of integrating new believers into the community of faith. Any church committed to making followers of Jesus will sooner or later have to deal with the likes of Boy Genius and the Virgin Mary – better start sooner rather than later, in my book.

---

[4] This is adapted from a phrase by Madeleine Delbrêl who says, 'the good news was not made for those on a quest, but for those disciples willing to obey'. Madeleine Delbrêl, *Nous Autres, Gens des Rues* (Paris: Éditions du Seuil, 1966), p73. Translated and paraphrased by Glyn Jones.

3

Free Hugs

He doesn't need us ... He just likes us.

If you are not familiar with the Free Hugs campaign, it was started back in the 1990s by an Australian[5] and made famous by the band Sick Puppies. It basically involved a guy holding up a 'Free Hugs' sign in a busy shopping area. The response was unprecedented. It surprised many people by its simplicity and the willingness of complete strangers to embrace in public. It says something of the times in which we live and our desperate need for connection with one another. Despite all our friends on Facebook, such real-life connection has taken a hit in recent times.

I watched the clip with friends back in 2006 and it reminded us of the words in the prodigal son passage in Luke's Gospel, chapter 15:

---

[5] https://www.freehugscampaign.org/ (accessed 20th November 2018).

But while he was still a long way off, his father saw him and was filled with compassion for him; he ran to his son, threw his arms round him and kissed him.
Luke 15:20

We felt that it captured beautifully how God feels about His children, and for me it was a simple picture of how God is longing to connect with us all.

A few months later I accompanied my friend Chris to an ex-mining town in the North, where he was doing balloon modelling as a form of street evangelism. Frankly, I am not very good at balloon modelling and all my attempts always end up looking a little obscene, so I thought I would give this one a miss. As I wandered about town and watched the troubled faces of the people, my mind wandered back to the Free Hugs clip. Granted, I wasn't on my home turf, which can have its advantages, such as not looking a complete idiot in front of people you know. However, this seemed a fairly tough place, and looking at the stern faces made me question how well free hugs would be received. After a lengthy period of procrastination and a hunt for a marker pen and a cardboard sign, I decided to give it a go.

I stood in a busy main street, with groups of men arguing emphatically outside a pub and charity sellers plying their trade. Suddenly, it seemed tense, unfriendly and even a bit dangerous. Maybe this *was* a bad idea. I looked down slowly at my sign and looked up to heaven and said a little prayer. And then, with all the courage I could muster, I raised the sign above my head: 'Free Hug'.

Immediately, I disappeared. It was as if I had suddenly become invisible. People walked past me and almost through me, as if there was nothing there. No one reacted, and everyone seemed to avert their gaze. There was not even a glimmer of acknowledgement in their faces that there was a strange guy holding a strange sign in the middle of the street. My confidence plummeted and, just as I was about to drop the sign and retreat, it got even worse. Four pub doormen dressed in black bomber jackets *had* been observing and they came over and surrounded me.

'What are you, some kind of pervert?' said one, as he poked me in the chest.

I stammered, and my legs went to jelly. I thought about coshing the bouncer with the sign and making a dash for it, but then the miracle happened – God sent four angels.

At that moment, four girls came over, dressed in pink shiny jackets. If you know the film *Grease*, then think Pink Ladies. They looked like the Pink Ladies but for me they were the Pink Angels. They were doing a promo for a local radio station and had seen the incident developing. One of them pushed forward and, poking the bouncer in the chest, said to him, 'What's your problem? Give him a hug!'

The others chipped in: 'Leave him alone, you bully!'

He had no chance, and before long the four bouncers all piled in to give me a hug, followed by the Pink Angels. That was all I needed to set me off, and I never looked back.

That afternoon, I hugged more than 250 people in two hours, and chatted with scores of people about the story of God and the prodigal son. In the past twelve years, my friends and I have used this to connect thousands of people with God. I am grateful to the guy whose idea it was, but I am mostly thankful for the angels who encouraged me that day.

On a subsequent occasion, I was working with a university chaplaincy, giving free hugs on campus. It was a busy day and there was a collection of huggers and watchers milling around, and several conversations happening. Amid the watchers, there was a group of Asian guys looking on. They stayed for quite a while and seemed intrigued, watching the spectacle. I went over to speak with them. They were exchange students from India and they wanted to know what it was about. I told them the story of the prodigal son.

They didn't seem particularly impressed with this concept and one asked me, 'Is your God all-powerful?'

'Yes,' I replied, 'I believe He is.'

'Then why does He need you to do His marketing for Him?'

Pause. I had no answer. He smiled at me, knowingly, as if to say, 'Do you see what I mean?'

I did.

I looked around at the people having fun with the free hugs, and their laughs and smiles. I had no pre-packed theological answer to give him. I looked back at my Indian friend and then said something I didn't even realise myself – the response came from my heart, rather than my head.

'He doesn't need us,' I said. 'I think He just likes us.'
We both looked at each other, a little puzzled.

As I reflect back on those words, I realise their truth for me. God does not need us any more than I need my five-year-old daughter to help me mow the grass. In fact, you could argue that it may be a whole heap easier for God to let people know about Himself without us. However, the reality is that we are a family and our heavenly Father invites us to take part in His business. Part of His business is reminding people of who He is and how He feels about His children, which, for me, is good news. We often, clearly, don't do the work that well; just as my daughter often creates more work when she helps me in the garden. But there is something wonderful about being with someone you love and who loves you and going about their business with them. That is why we are all invited into doing God's marketing.

I realise that Free Hugs is not everyone's cup of tea. But before you drown the enthusiasm of free huggers, remember that we all need encouragement sometimes. It is easy to find fault and extinguish a willingness to try new things out. Sometimes, a small word of encouragement can release others with the courage to step out in bringing hope and good news. By taking a few risks like this, new ideas are born and old ones are refashioned in novel and creative ways. There is a reason that 'angel' features in the word 'evangelism'. An angel is a messenger. What kind of messenger are you with your friends? Can I encourage you to be a messenger of encouragement for others? In doing so, you will create a ripple in the water, and enough ripples will become a wave of good news.

4

Cans of Lager

Occasionally, I lead people to Jesus. But as a general rule, Jesus leads me to people.

I had spent all day lecturing a group of students on the willingness to 'share the hope we have'[6] with others. We had done a Bible study, the rationale, the theory and the risk assessment and wrapped it all up in a tidy prayer – job well done. I headed home on my bike. It was a gentle seven-mile ride down one of those recommissioned railway tracks which took me past the cemetery, through a big housing estate and then on into the open country. It was late afternoon and, after being with people all day, I was looking forward to the peace of my own thoughts.

As I pedalled along, I spied a guy ahead of me carrying two white shopping bags. He was walking with his back to me, but I could see from his stoop that his bags were

---

[6] See 1 Peter 3:15.

heavy. He had at least another half a mile to walk before the next exit and something about his faltering pace moved me. I thought of the words of Jesus, 'Come to Me, all you who … are heavy laden, and I will give you rest.'[7]

I considered what we had been discussing that day, the readiness to share the hope we have, and so I decided to do the easy thing: I committed this stranger to prayer as I cycled home. As I drifted past, I saw that his shopping bags were full of cans of lager. Everything about the guy – the way he walked, his demeanour, his head stooped low and the look on his face – spoke of a grey cloud following him around. And so I stopped.

I didn't know how to start, so I didn't try too hard – I just told him that I saw a grey cloud following him and asked him how he was doing. He seemed to find this a welcome interruption, and he put his bags down and stretched his arms. He didn't find my question odd at all, and with a fragile confidence, described some of the relationship difficulties he was having, how life was bearing down on him at the moment, although he was hoping things would improve. He smiled at the grey cloud idea and said that it was fitting. I shared about my faith and how I need God when life bears down on me. I offered to pray for him and we shared a short but sincere prayer for help together, there and then. After encouraging each other, we waved one another off and I carried on down the cycle track.

If I am honest, I felt good about myself. I probably felt a bit smug, if the truth be known. Good job, Jones! I had

---

managed to practise what I had been preaching all day, no fuss, no bother, and no bright lights. Simple and real. I ticked the evangelism box for the day and sped off home.

I went past the cemetery, through the estate and saw the fields ahead opening up as dusk began to descend. There are usually more people on the track the nearer to town you are, but as you go out into the countryside you usually just meet the occasional Lycra-clad cyclist speeding past. This was precisely the reason why my attention was drawn to another figure in the distance walking towards me, from the countryside. There was something strangely familiar about this guy, and as we approached each other I saw he too had a carrier bag, bulging with cans. I sped past.

This guy was walking with more determination than the first guy and didn't appear to have a grey cloud following him. Probably trying to get home before dark. I sped on.

As I headed into the green belt, a troublesome thought buzzed into my head: did Jesus tick a box for the day and head home? Leper healed, time for tea? Feed the 5,000, then home to watch *Coronation Street*? I'm not sure He went about His day with a to-do list, and so I wondered to myself, why stop for one person but not for two? I reminded myself of the prayer with the first guy and tried to reassure my gnawing doubt with a dose of self-appeasement.

But every yard I cycled, the thought became more and more uncomfortable. Sometimes, the more we try to reason something, the more unreasonable it becomes. By this time, it was nearly dark, but I knew in my heart that I had to at least go back and give it a try. Reluctantly, I drew to a halt. Looking around the fields, I turned around and headed back the way I had come.

As I cycled back through the fields and towards the town, I hoped in my heart that this guy would not be there and that he had made it home. At least then I'd be able to answer my conscience and God that I had shown willing. But that was not to be. A mile or so later, I spied the figure walking in the same determined fashion. I began to rehearse what I would say in my head. How I would explain why I had cycled past him and then come back. The more I rehearsed, the more ridiculous it got, and I started to tie myself up in knots. I eventually gave up and resigned myself simply to offering a prayer to the guy. However, it was not to be, and a truly agonising moment ensued.

I pulled up and confidently addressed him.

'I'm just cycling home and saying some prayers. Anything I can keep you in my prayers for?'

He looked down at my feet and, slowly, in a resolute manner, moved his gaze up my body until he stared at me, square in the eyes.

What he actually replied is unprintable here. But let's just imagine he told me to 'go away'. Then he turned and carried on walking.

I stood there, motionless.

I watched him march on into the dusk and out of sight. He didn't look back.

Slowly, I turned my bike and pedalled off, still in a daze. My mood went from fury, to feeling rejected, to sulking. I cursed the man, cursed God, cursed my bike and finally cursed myself for being such a dipstick: I could have got myself seriously beaten up there, I thought. Finally, I just cycled back through the fields in the darkness, feeling hollow. Then a strange thing happened.

It was as if God smiled at me in amusement. I scowled back at Him. His smile then turned to affectionate laughter and my scowl turned to a reluctant smile. I truly felt like God couldn't help laughing at me and what had just happened. It *was* kind of funny, I suppose. And then I experienced the wonderful, irreverent amusement of the Almighty. The God who had thoughtfully challenged me not to be a box-ticking Christian was now laughing at me and I started to laugh, too. And we laughed and laughed all the way home.

Occasionally, I lead people to Jesus. But as a general rule, Jesus leads me to people. What happens then is not always what I expect. But when I hear Him and follow Him, I once again become the person I am supposed to be on this desperate planet – fully human and fully me.

Being who you are made to be is easier said than done for most of us. I don't know about you, but I spend a fair amount of my time trying to be someone I'm not. Someone cleverer, someone funnier, someone more popular, and so on. And in doing so, I often live a half version of my real self. There is actually one person who managed to live a full version of themselves – a full human being – and that is Jesus. Fully God and fully human.

I saw an advert on a bus recently, which argued that there is a good reason why there is only one version of you. And it's true – when you are fully you and I am fully me, which can only happen in God, people will see, hear and experience Jesus. They may not like it, but they will perceive it. St Irenaeus writes, 'The glory of God is a human being fully alive.'[8] Being fully alive doesn't mean being active, successful and living your dreams, as advertisers would have us believe. It means being you, warts and all. Sometimes being you is ordinary, shy, stupid, funny, clever, and so on. I'm not suggesting you be who I am – that's my shape. And for me, to be fully alive in God involves me juggling my stupidity, my pride, my flawed reasoning and my willingness to try.

In doing this, we get a taste of true integrity. We also experience a wholeness with God in which His affection for us, His children, becomes felt and known. In our efforts to be ourselves, just occasionally, we may genuinely make Him laugh. And if we can just manage to stop taking ourselves so seriously, we may have the opportunity to laugh with Him.

[8] Irenaeus of Lyon (n.d.), Christian Classics Ethereal Library, http://www.ccel.org/ccel/schaff/anf01.toc.html (accessed 22nd November 2018).

5

Pastor Benny

More people glanced around the room. And then it slowly began to dawn on me. They were all waiting – and waiting for me.

My first official visit to church as a fully fledged Christian was, truthfully, a bit of a nightmare. I had not been to a place where people willingly chose to express their faith publicly for a long time, so I wasn't quite sure what to expect. It was in *the* roughest neighbourhood in town, and as I wandered past boarded-up terraced houses decorated with graffiti, I saw the church I was looking for – it looked as dingy as the ramshackle street in which it stood. It had nothing to endear it to people except for a shiny new A-frame sign announcing the service, which looked oddly out of place in this dilapidated neighbourhood.

I was greeted at the door of a small whitewashed warehouse by an American, wearing a clean, brightly coloured suit and what I swear was an excess of hair dye and fake tan. He waved a hand towards me and introduced himself, with a Texan twang, as Pastor Benny.[9] His tanned hand shook mine enthusiastically. I gulped; this was a bit surreal.

'Hi, I'm Glyn, nice to meet you, Benny,' I replied, as I tried to extricate myself from his vice-like grip.

He forced a smile. '*Pastor* Benny,' he repeated.

'Nice to meet you, Benny,' I too repeated.

'*Pastor* Benny.' His intonation rose, and his teeth gritted behind the smile. His hold on my hand intensified.

I groaned deep in my soul as distant memories of irate people pretending to be nice murmured to my subconscious memory, 'Welcome back to church.'

Had God not recently become a very real part of my life, I would have turned around and left then. But I didn't. I knew that God was very real and, somehow, I knew that this was a place where people believed the same thing. So I wrenched myself free, forced a smile and walked in.

I was not ready for what greeted me. I was well aware this was unlikely to be a choral evensong, but what met me was a tidal wave of sound. There were about twenty people in the small warehouse all shouting eagerly to each other, trying to hold conversations over a cacophony of noise emanating from a distorted keyboard and a slightly crazed-looking drummer. All seemed unaware of the hullabaloo they were making. I snuck in and sat down.

---

[9] Not his real name.

Fortunately, no one spoke to me, and Pastor Benny came in promptly and made his way to the front. His arrival brought an end to the pandemonium and people reverently sat down and all shouting stopped. Then *he* started shouting.

I'm still not sure why, but for a small room of twenty people, he saw the need to use amplification fitting for a small football stadium. And, as if the speakers weren't functioning properly, he shouted emphatically at us for over an hour. He seemed to think there was a direct correlation between sheer volume and pleasing God. If so, then the Almighty must have been delighted that day. For the record, I wish I had been up there with Him – with earplugs.

I was not used to sitting in one place and listening to someone shout for over an hour. For the final twenty minutes, I was planning my exit – how to stand up, smile, and get out of there quickly. And then Pastor Benny paused, and cast his gaze across the room. I'm sure he sensed people were going to make a run for it.

'Is there anyone here present who would like to give their life to Jesus Christ this very night?'

Silence. Clearly, nobody did.

'Is there anyone here present who would like to give their life to Jesus Christ this very night?' he repeated, with exactly the same Southern drawl.

Nope. Never mind, I thought. They're all probably deaf and didn't hear you.

He asked again: 'Is there anyone here present who would like to give their life to Jesus this very night?'

All quiet – you could have heard a pin drop. I desperately wanted to look around, but dared not.

Someone shifted uncomfortably behind me, but no one budged.

He was holding the moment, letting people work it through in their minds.

Eventually, people started to glance around furtively, one at a time. I made eye contact with a few sympathetic faces and we each gave each other a knowing look. More people glanced around the room. And then it slowly began to dawn on me. They were all waiting – and waiting for *me*.

Now, *I* shifted uncomfortably. I eyed the door and calculated the distance. I smiled back, nervously, at them – I was a goner. I knew God was real, there was no question about that, and church had seemed the next logical step, but this was not what I had signed up for. I wondered why they were all looking at me with such desperate concern. I mused that they were all probably just hoping that someone would stand up and put an end to the supplications of the preacher. As I stared back, unsure what to do, somebody came up and took me by the arm and led me to the front of the stage. They didn't ask me if I wanted to go and, like a fool, I followed and knelt down. I was petrified.

I was asked whether I would like to read a prayer confessing my sin and my need for forgiveness and a saviour. I politely declined and informed the person that God and I were getting along quite well for the moment, but thanked them for their concern.

This was not going to dissuade my desperate companion. He asked me again with a pleading look in his eye. I politely declined a second time. I may be wrong, but at this point I sensed the drawing near of other concerned souls. The pack was closing in. I realised then that I was probably not going to get out alive.

On the third request, I informed my concerned colleagues that I would say their prayer, *if* it made them feel better, to which they eagerly nodded. I looked up and felt God smile at me and I mumbled their prayer, begrudgingly. Thinking this would suffice, I stood to retake my seat. But my newly found friends had other ideas. One dragged me back down to my knees and pleaded for my full name, address and personal details. Enough was enough. I didn't smile back. I took my coat and left.

I believe the good news of Jesus Christ is something like this: we have left God and chosen to do things our own way or someone else's way. I believe that this has separated us from God. But somehow, God became human and that God-man, Jesus, died on a cross, paying the penalty for our selfish lives. I believe that He rose again from the dead and that those who choose to follow Him as their God rise into a new life as spiritual people and children of God. That is good news! But that first day in church as a new believer, I was not in a place to grasp all that.

My friend Chris writes that 'good news needs to be understood as good news, otherwise it is no news and no news is bad news'.[10] That day, I experienced it as bad news. It is not that the message of sin, forgiveness and new life is bad news; it's just that no one thought to ask where I was at before they led me down the aisle. That day I desperately wanted to meet some other people who also believed in God. I didn't need theology; I needed Christian company. That was what made it bad news for me that day.

The good news is not a formula, a script or even a theology. The good news is a person, Jesus. The Word of God is a person, Jesus: 'the Word became flesh and dwelt among us'.[11] Because the good news is a person, it is alive, dynamic and active. While it never changes, how it relates to people constantly does. The moment we attempt to box a person into a neat formula, the good news loses its personality and becomes two-dimensional, grey and tired.

Because the good news is the person, when we reject the things that Jesus says, so we reject the Jesus who says them. As we accept the things that He says, so we accept Him. And to accept Him means to follow Him. Following is a journey that leads to places and encounters beyond our horizons, but the good news journey always starts where our need is most pressing.

Some journeys start in captivity and the first stage is freedom; others start in a meaningless existence and the initial destination is one of purpose. Yet others start in

---

[10] This is a quote that Chris Duffett often uses in his teaching and can be found in his first book, *Smack Heads and Fat Cats* (West Knapton: Gilead Books, 2009), p121.
[11] John 1:14, NKJV.

guilt and the journey is one of forgiveness and a new start. Eventually, they all lead, as the old hymn goes, to a 'green hill far away, Without a city wall, Where the dear Lord was crucified, Who died to save us all'.[12] We will all come to that cross eventually, but we don't all start there. The good news journey is one we do not walk alone, and eventually we find all those things along the way, because meaning, purpose and freedom all belong to the person of Jesus Christ. All of these things are part of the personality of Jesus – the question is: where do you begin?

Evangelism, for me, is about where we start. It is about people experiencing the reality of Jesus Christ beginning where *they* are at, not where you or I want them to be. If you live in a chaotic society, order makes sense to you; if you are trapped in addiction, freedom is the start; if you walk under the weight of guilt, then forgiveness is the way in. If you want to know where to start in evangelism, then ask yourself the question: who am I talking to?

This makes the good news vibrant and adaptable. It makes every encounter with people unique, and our privilege becomes to walk people to a place with God that neither of us has visited before[13] – it is not a destination, but the beginning of an adventure with a person who calls Himself *The Way*.

---

[12] Cecil Frances Alexander (1818–95),
https://www.hymnal.net/en/hymn/h/995 (accessed 15th November 2018).

[13] An idea paraphrased from Vincent Donovan in his book *Christianity Rediscovered: An Epistle from the Masai* (London: SCM, 1978), p. xix, preface to the second edition.

6

The Car Auction

*The key ingredient to a true missional lifestyle? It should feel
like your own shoes you are walking in.*

We needed a new car – quickly. Our faithful runaround
was showing worrying signs of giving up the ghost and
the splendour of our 1.4 diesel Vauxhall Corsa was
fading, rapidly. While I admire the faith heavyweights
whom God answers miraculously with unexpected gifts
and brown paper envelopes through the door, we weren't
there. God works with us where we are, and I am grateful
for that. We were skint, we needed a new car and we
didn't have the faith for greater things, so I went to the
car auction to buy an old banger.

It was a jostling, noisy place, with engines revving and
local mavericks frowning as they inspected cars and
kicked tyres on the car park. I had no idea what to do, so I
joined in the frowning and kicking of tyres. It was a
miserable, wet autumn evening and so, after mooching

around, I made my way into the hangar where the cars were brought for the auction. Inside I found a heady hustle and bustle of people chatting away and trying to make themselves heard over the cacophony of the auctioneer shouting out meaningless numbers. It was a strange place for me, and I was acutely aware of not knowing how things worked. This is what church must feel like for a new visitor.

Bemused, I decided to head for the food counter and do the one thing I knew how to do – buy some food. It was a small counter serving basic, cheap and cheerful British heart disease on a plate. I smiled at the jolly-looking lady, leaned into the counter and ordered some chips.

'How's *your* day going?' I enquired.

She paused, and looked up at me from the fryer. A slight tilt of her head and the pause betrayed a subtle moment of confusion.

I figured she mustn't get many people asking and was processing the kindness of this stranger. She re-engaged with me and smiled.

'Great, yes, good.' She became more animated as her answer unfolded. 'Really good,' she replied.

'Brilliant,' I responded.

Silence.

I waited for my chips.

'He's got two now, you know,' she continued.

'Two,' I repeated, pretending to understand. Did she just say, 'He's got two now'? Two what? I thought to myself. It was now my turn to be confused. I mentally repeated her sentence in my head and smiled like a fool at her.

'Yeah, and Karen's fine too, got a new job,' she continued.

'New job,' I repeated, and laughed nervously as if that was in some way funny. Then I nodded, thinking, what on earth is she talking about?

She carried on, 'They're in Milton Keynes now, you know?'

'No way,' I replied. 'Who would have ever thought it, Milton Keynes.' I was starting to panic in my head.

It is an odd feeling to be conducting a conversation with a person about a subject that is clearly heartfelt for them and simultaneously nonsense for yourself. I was aware of a creeping sense of unease. I had come over to the food counter because I had felt out of place and out of my comfort zone. I had come to do something familiar, buy some food, but even this simple transaction was proving tricky.

I was also aware of a minor moral dilemma. I had no idea what this lady was talking about, but she seemed genuinely happy to be talking about it. It seemed unfair to cut her short but wrong to go on feigning interest – I believe the technical term is 'bluffing'.

As she continued speaking in animated tones and enthusiastic mannerisms, I realised that my food was going to take longer than I had hoped. I mentally calculated the depth of the hole I was digging myself into, and the high probability that I would soon be found out. And so I bit the bullet.

'Sorry,' I interrupted, coyly, 'I don't mean to be rude ...' and then I quickly blurted out, 'but I have no idea what you are talking about.'

She stopped dead, and gave me a puzzled stare.

She tilted her head again, in the same way she had previously done.

'Dave,' she said. 'Dave!' she repeated.

'Dave? Who's Dave?' I appealed.

'Why, my son, of course!' She looked genuinely surprised that I should not know her son personally.

'Right.' I hovered, unsure where this was going. Once again, as is often the case in my life, time seemed to roll on in slow motion, and I felt like a spectator. Why did I come to this auction, how does this all work and why can't I just buy some food without making a scene?

Reality clicked back into place.

'You just asked me about Dave,' she said.

My mind replayed the conversation in 'fast-backward'.

I couldn't place it. I looked round for the exit and got ready to run.

You asked me, 'How's your Dave going?'

I paused, and the penny dropped.

'Noooooo, no, no nooooo,' I smiled. 'How's your *day* going?' I said, slowly and clearly above the noise of the auction.

'Ooooooh!' She and I both burst out laughing simultaneously.

Suddenly this alien place became familiar again and the connection between two human beings was made.

I think that as human beings we are wired for real connection with other people. When we lose that, we feel isolated and alien, and we no longer behave as we are designed to. Simple interactions get tricky.

I was doing some training recently and, at the beginning of one of the sessions, one of the guys, who had years of experience under his belt, said, 'I just want to know how to do "comfortable evangelism", evangelism that feels like me.' He had done all the courses and heard all the training, but it still felt like he was wearing someone else's shoes.

While I am not sure that evangelism will always be comfortable, I understand what he meant. He wanted to be himself and connect with people in a way that fitted him, not me or some other person. I think it is ultimately very possible. So what is the key ingredient to a true missional lifestyle? It should feel like your *own* shoes you are walking in.

We are all different and have our unique gifts and talents, along with our own personal challenges to face. While our lives are all infinitely different, I think there are two habits that we can all develop which lend themselves to 'more comfortable' evangelism: *intention* and *attention*. I'll come back to *intention* in chapter 9, but developing *attention* is a worthwhile habit that we can all think about. Paying attention to people makes you aware of them, aware of God and ultimately aware of yourself, and often leads to a more natural way of sharing faith. The book of James tells us 'be quick to listen, slow to speak'.[14] A while

---

14 James 1:19.

ago, I gave some thought to how I may do this in my own life and so I decided, among other things, to ask people I met how their day was going – and then to genuinely listen to them, whatever they wanted to say.

In reality, people often just say 'good' or seem surprised and answer politely, but each week I listen to people who want to talk, whether in shops, at the swimming pool, buying petrol or waiting at the school gate. I have sat and cried with people losing loved ones, been bemused and confused by the mess of strangers' lives, and every now and then, laughed with them and told them about the 'hope I have'.

I'll offer to pray with people or tell them about God, not because I have to or I have a script, but because they want me to. Ultimately, people are interested in a God who is interested in them. I am not suggesting that you do this – these are my shoes to walk in – but I am suggesting that you find your own ways of paying attention to the people you meet every day in a purposeful way.

Another way I do this is by forcing myself to stop when I feel prompted by God, and taking stock of the moment. I'll literally stop walking, cycling or driving and listen to the sounds, smell the air and watch the details. A particular way I do this is by retracing my steps. I'll be heading somewhere and I will stop and go back a bit, then walk the steps again, but this time paying attention to where I am and what God may be showing me. It drives my wife mad, and the kids think it's hilarious because it often makes me late for things. A Buddhist friend of mine calls it *mindfulness*; I call it prayerfulness.

Mindfulness is powerful in tuning yourself into your surroundings and yourself, but it centres on *you*, and its ultimate destination without God is loneliness. Prayerfulness is about listening, being in the moment and heightening your awareness of God speaking through all things, including the people you meet – *its* ultimate goal is relationship and company. To be fully aware will never mean solitude, but an awareness of the presence of God in all things. Developing your own ways of *attention* make for a missional lifestyle, one where you are in tune with the Spirit of God wherever you are.

And so, in a missional life, prayer is not necessarily a long list of things that we want God to do for us, but a way of tuning into God that allows us to see ordinary situations differently. Madeleine Delbrêl suggests that prayer is often about the things that we decide not to do, or to do with a different slant.[15] Making small adjustments to our ordinary, everyday lives opens opportunities that we don't usually perceive and tend to overlook, because we assume each situation is predictable. Taking the ordinary things that we do naturally and doing them prayerfully can be a novel way to wear in a new pair of shoes and make them fit like your own.

---

[15] Madeleine Delbrêl, *La Joie de Croire* (Paris: Éditions du Seuil, 1968), p257.

7

The Football Match

Courage, intellect, charisma and a dose of the 'slightly odd' are not required skills for evangelism. An open and willing heart is.

Summer was here. Exams were over, essays submitted and students sat around leisurely on the university field, chatting and fooling around before they each headed their respective ways. Some were off to festivals, others to summer jobs and others to travel the world. There were hugs and waves as friends promised to keep in touch over the summer and beyond. A friend and I were kicking around a football on the university field. We were working alongside the chaplains, which, that afternoon, meant simply hanging out with people.

Before long, a group of about twelve lads arrived and commandeered the field for a football match. One strolled over to us and asked if we wanted to join them as they were a few men short. We looked at each other – this seemed a most appropriate way to be a chaplain. We played for a little less than an hour. I was the mature member of the team and when someone suggested a half-time break, I approved enthusiastically. We all meandered over to one of the goal areas and sat down. While maybe not all best friends, these boys all knew each other, and they sat as one big group in a circle together on the grass. We sat with them.

A few showed a mild interest in us and asked us a few questions. One of them asked me if I was a student and I told him that I was a lecturer.

'In what?' he asked.

A second before, the group were chatting and animated. But as he asked that question, it seemed that the chatting hushed and the group fell silent. It was a simple question, but a surreal moment. It seemed as if not only the circle of lads, but also the whole field, had fallen quiet in anticipation of my answer.

Pause.

'Theology and Eeeshlism,' I mumbled. The word didn't form properly in my mouth.

Pause.

'Eeeshlism,' I repeated. It was like I was drugged or had just visited the dentist and my mouth was numb, incapable of forming the words.

A circle of sweaty footballers looked completely blank. *'What?'* came a chorus of incredulous voices.

'Evagism,' I tried again.

They started to frown, and I could feel the tension rise. All eyes were on me.

The word formed in my belly in a cocktail of fear, frustration and panic, and flooded up into my vocal chords ...

'EVANGELISM!' I blurted out, as if by shouting it would flow more easily.

Now the whole field actually did look over.

Blank faces circled me, with eyebrows beginning to furrow.

Silence. It was as if a tumbleweed had blown through the group and away over the field.

'Evangelism,' I said again, quietly, as I regained my composure. 'Evangelism?' one guy repeated, with a genuinely shocked tone that made me wince.

'Yes,' I apologised.

The group looked on.

'What on *earth* is that?' asked another member of the group, with disbelief.

I mumbled and bumbled an explanation – something about theology, God, faith, Church – but I could see the confusion growing and so I swallowed hard.

'It's about Jesus,' I said, almost regretfully. 'Yes,' I repeated as if to myself, quietly, as though all alone, 'It's all about Jesus.'

It is moments like that when I wish I were a plumber or an architect.

'I am a plumber; I fix taps, sinks and kitchens. You name it, I fix it.' I would feel normal and a bit less of an odd bod.

The group stared at me, clearly taken aback by the word 'Jesus'.

Some of the group scowled, as if I had just betrayed our fledgling friendship; others just stared. No one said anything. It was as if there were a six-week pause before conversations picked up slowly again. There was no recognition of the scene that had taken place. No one said anything, and we all pretended that nothing had just happened. It was awkward.

I remember telling this story once to a group of church ministers and seeing the look of disdain on some of their faces.

'Why are you embarrassed about being a Christian?' they quizzed me, in the safe confines of a Christian conference centre. Clearly none of them had stooped that low.

The word 'evangelism' has had a bad press. It can conjure up images of preachers fleecing folk out of their hard-earned savings, zealous people knocking at your door, the angry street preacher or the 'End of the world is nigh' sandwich-board man. Unsurprisingly, announce a bit of evangelism at your local church and you'll soon find the pews empty, except for an odd-looking bunch twitching eagerly at the back – for the record, I am probably one of them!

Even for those who never visit churches and whose collective memory no longer stretches that far back, evangelism rings of over-the-top-ness. In business, it refers to developing a culture of zealous people who will advocate strongly for your product and try to convince others to buy and use it. It has echoes of manipulation, marketing and hype.

If you weren't already aware, evangelism is not currently *all the rage* among Christians. A cursory glance at book titles online will reveal prayer, discipleship and worship much higher up the list. Many of us feel unqualified – we don't know how to explain our faith and certainly aren't sure of the all the answers. What about when our friends, families and work colleagues bring up the hot potatoes of evolution, sexuality or other religions, not to mention the scandals that have littered Church history, ancient and modern? We are frightened of being offensive in a politically correct world, being misunderstood, misleading people or being ridiculed. Many of us don't fit the persona of outgoing, wacky characters who can chat to anyone. If this is you, then rest reassured, *you're* the normal one and you are in good company.

If evangelism is purely about accosting strangers out of the blue, then it is an activity for the bold or foolish. If evangelism is only about giving a reasoned explanation of the Christian message in clear and coherent terms, then it remains the territory of a few gifted writers and orators – and the rest of us are off the hook! Not only do such understandings of evangelism narrow the full dimension of the good news, but they disqualify the vast majority of ordinary Christians living out their ordinary lives. Courage, intellect, charisma and a dose of the 'slightly odd' are not required skills for evangelism. An open and willing heart is.

An open and willing heart like that of Mary, the mother of Jesus, is like a lump of clay that God can mould. And, given the opportunity, He will mould your heart into a shape that reflects you. Evangelism will sound like you and look like you, and the Church will acquire a new colour in its palette, rather than us all being shades of the same. So maybe we need to try laying down our preconceptions of evangelism, and start with a willingness to learn again who we are and how we can *be the light*.[16]

The word 'Jesus', however, has always had a mixed reception. Sometimes, we are embarrassed about Jesus. I am sometimes embarrassed about following Him and I'm embarrassed about letting others know about Him.

I am woefully familiar with the verse 'whoever disowns me before others, I will disown before my Father in heaven'.[17] But just before you consign me to the heresy heap, I am not the first, or the last. In fact, one of the first was the disciple Peter, who denied knowing Jesus three times before the cock crowed.[18] And look what he went on to do! Despite all that, I am glad that I follow Jesus.

Whether you teach evangelism or you are a plumber, a minister or a mum, the issue remains the same for all of us: the name of Jesus is a challenge. The name of Jesus has always and will always mean something – it literally means 'the LORD saves' and it should provoke a reaction in everyone who hears it or says it. Some parts of the Eastern Orthodox Church consider the presence of God to reside in the name 'Jesus'. Whether you believe that or not, it implies in its very nature that we are people in need of God.

---

[16] A favourite phrase of my friend Chris Duffett.

[17] Matthew 10:33.

[18] Luke 22:54-62.

The name 'Jesus' is not our property. It does not belong to us and it is true that we have no need to apologise or justify Jesus – He is who He is. Depending on where you are at, that is good news or bad news, a fresh breeze or a bad stench.[19] To lack food, shelter and companionship is a burden shared by all the animal kingdom – to lack God is solely a human misery.[20] And unless people hear that name, Jesus, they will never awaken to the real Hope. So, whether plumber or lecturer, minister or mum, be encouraged to share that name openly and freely. But, if like me, or Peter the fisherman, you get it all wrong regularly, then take heart. Jesus met Peter on a beach and walked him back, arm in arm, asking him a question. Not 'are you good at this' or 'why did you mess that up?' but quite simply 'do you love me?'.[21]

---

[19] 2 Corinthians 2:15-16: 'For we are the aroma of Christ to God among those who are being saved and among those who are perishing, to one a fragrance from death to death, to the other a fragrance from life to life' (ESV).

[20] This is a reworded sentiment expressed by Madeleine Delbrêl, *Nous Autres, Gens des Rue*, p23. Translated and paraphrased by Glyn Jones. It has also been expressed by many other Christians down the ages, famously worded by St Augustine of Hippo: 'Thou hast made us for thyself, O Lord, and our heart is restless until it finds its rest in thee', https://www.goodreads.com/quotes/42572-thou-hast-made-us-for-thyself-o-lord-and-our (accessed 22nd November 2018).

[21] John 21:17.

8

The Man with the Snood

So much of our time as Church is spent worrying about how to reach people, when each day hundreds of people reach us; unfortunately, we don't see them.

I love my snood. If you don't know what a snood is, it is like a scarf, but trendier. Well, that's what I like to think. My wife knitted mine and it's a prized object. I got the idea from a guy I met on the street – the man with the snood.

I had been with a group of students that day and we had been discussing how the early British Celts and the disciples of Jesus shared an apparent willingness to go, leave their comfort zones and be prepared to engage with people as they encountered them on the road. So we concluded that this was the true heart of the New Testament word *apostolos*, which we often translate as 'mission'. The literal meaning of the word is 'sent'. It had been a long day and, after these lengthy discussions, there was just one thing left to do: if we were the people who were *sent*, then we needed to *go*.

I suggested we pray together, then head into town with no specific destination and see where God would take us. I was aware of the apprehension in the room, as they thought this was a sit-down lecture. They were wrong – this was a practical! I asked the students if we could try just following our noses but avoiding any attempts to initiate conversations with people. Naturally, we weren't going to ignore people if they spoke to us (that would be too weird), but would not go looking for encounters. This seemed to reassure the group and so we headed off.

We meandered down the high street like a group of tourists, with nobody saying a word – not even to each other, which seemed a little too focused. Not 500 yards from the classroom, we were approached by two guys. They were hipsters: skinny jeans, trendy trainers, funky haircuts and an amazing piece of knitwear around one guy's neck – the snood. He introduced himself as a local hairdresser and explained that they were hunting for a model on whom to do a cut. I blushed and felt a little flattered until he explained that Jess, one of the students with long, dark hair, fitted the bill precisely. 'Of course,' I mumbled, a little embarrassed, and took a small step back.

They addressed Jess and asked if she would be willing to be the model. Jess immediately beamed and straightened up, but then she paused and slumped back a little. She replied that she probably couldn't go with them because she was in a lecture. The two guys looked puzzled.

'A lecture?' the man with the snood laughed. 'What kind of a lecture is this?' They were jovial and clearly enjoyed the intrigue.

Jess pointed at me and said, 'Ask him, he's the lecturer.'

I took my small step forward again.

I explained to the man with the snood that this was a theology lecture looking to explore how faith might relate to people who don't call themselves Christians.

He listened with a generous smile on his face, apparently not knowing if we were pulling his leg or if we were part of a religious cult. He was clearly a playful chap and I suggested that he could have my student if he were willing to take part in the lecture. He agreed without hesitation.

I asked him about the snood and he let me try it on. He asked us about our faith and so we told him. He found our relationship with God curious and endearing but, as we went on, you could see something was bothering him. The objection eventually bubbled up to the surface.

With a hint of regret, he pointed out that while this sounded interesting, it was not for him, because he was gay. Rather than enlighten him as to the theological and biblical perspectives on sexuality, the students rightly let him speak. He told us a little about his life. He was genuine, open and honest, and we were really taking a shine to this guy. One of the students offered to give him a Bible so he could make up his own mind. It was her prized Bible in leather-bound pink and he thought that was hilarious.

He had met his part of the deal, so I released Jess to the man with the snood. She was hopping with excitement and skipped away for a free cut and blow-dry with two of the coolest cats in town – students will do anything these days to get out of a lecture!

I think the whole group, myself included, had forgotten why we were actually in town that day and it was only walking back to the lecture room that we all realised what had happened. We had followed the command to *go*, and didn't need anything but the willingness to be interrupted. We had believed that God would lead us, and so He had.

Every day, people cross our paths and interrupt our plans, and most of the time we see them as an inconvenience. But what if we looked out for the signs of the Holy Spirit drifting across our paths and decided to be attentive? God might show us something about them. If part of prayer is listening to God, then a prayerful life is allowing God to speak, and He often does, through the interruptions. This is about practising 'interruptability' – the expectation that God is able to cross your path with people when least expected, if only you let Him.

In the ever-increasing hectic world in which we live, it is probably no bad thing that we are all seeking some quiet in our lives. Yoga, meditation and silent retreats are all big business as people try to curb the insatiable demands of modern life. Technology, 24/7 availability, family, and busier and busier lives all clamour for our attention. I am an introvert at heart and I love to get away regularly to hear God through the quiet. That said, I have a problem with it: I don't want to live my life on binges of reflection and quiet; what is more, most of my life is not like that.

Some of my friends don't have the luxury of going to a silent retreat, meditating three times a day or paying regular visits to their spiritual director. Holding down three jobs to pay the rent or taking care of a chronically ill family member excludes you from the popular spiritual cures available to the fortunate few.

So what does the psalm mean: 'Be still, and know that I am God'?[22]

Being truly still is not necessarily about silence or about sitting quietly – it is about moving in perfect unison with God and His world in motion. It is about resonating at the same frequency as the world around you and tuning into God as part of that. You can be still in a moving car, still on a jostling train, still walking down the streets or even still in a boat in a storm.[23] When you are still, interruptions become part of the movement and you become able to interact with them without them disrupting your journey. This is stillness. Interruptability for me is an example of stillness and dynamic peace.

It seems that we think of peace as a feeling to be found through things such as mediation, meditation or medication. While all of these are welcome and beneficial, they suppose that peace is an

---

[22] Psalm 46:10.

[23] See the account of Jesus asleep in the boat in Mark 4:35-41.

absence of problems, absence of conflict or, even better, absence of people. But true peace is not an absence of anything; it is the presence of a person, the presence of God.[24] As Paul writes to the church in Ephesus, 'For he himself is our peace'.[25]

We can recognise the peace of God and His stillness in busy everyday lives when we become willing and open to interruption. The disciples themselves were interrupted by the risen Jesus with the words 'Peace be with you!'[26] Peace was with them, literally, in the person of Jesus.

Jess looked a million dollars the next day and, as promised, the other student dropped off her favourite leather-bound pink Bible to the man with the snood – he received it gladly. Some of the students kept in touch with him and popped in to see him from time to time. Occasionally he would send us email updates with smiley faces. He was grateful for our prayers and thoughts.

The man with the snood had walked into our lives uninvited and unannounced. So much of our time as Church is spent worrying about how to reach people, when each day hundreds of people reach *us*; unfortunately, we don't see them. That day, thankfully, we were paying attention and were gifted with a

---

[24] This is an idea I have developed from Madeleine Delbrêl who writes that solitude is not the absence of people, but rather the presence of God, something which I find synonymous with peace. Madeleine Delbrêl, *Nous Autres, Gens des Rue*, pp29, 76. Translated and paraphrased by Glyn Jones.

[25] Ephesians 2:14.

[26] John 20:21.

friendship and a chance to share the reason for the hope that we have with a guy who thought that God's reach was not long enough for him.

Later that year I got an email from one of the students, which came as an abrupt shock. She had popped by to see the man with the snood, but he was not there. The staff didn't know how to tell her, but the man with the snood, in the prime of his life, proud owner of a pink Bible, had suddenly and without warning collapsed and died.

I honestly don't know where the man with the snood was in relation to God and faith. I wish I could say, but I can't. What I can say, however, is that I know that there is a God who calls out to *all* – whoever they are, wherever they are, however near or far they feel from Him. They will never know about God unless ordinary people living ordinary lives see the interruptions as part of God's plan.

72

9

The Peg and the Pumice Stone

Do the little things, the small things that you have heard and seen me do.
(St David of Wales)

I was rushing to get out of the house to catch my train. I was also shouting at everyone in range about someone having moved my keys. As I located my keys in the place *I* had left them, I grabbed two things lying next to the phone and shoved them in my bag: a clothes peg and a pumice stone. Goodness knows why there was a clothes peg and a pumice stone next to the phone that day. But anyone who has been to our house will know it is a bazaar of strange objects, mostly collected by my wife and carefully deposited at random places and intervals throughout the house. The pumice stone I can account for, as it was one of several lying around the house – souvenirs that we had brought back from a family holiday to Sicily. My daughter collected these stones and she had picked them up from the roadside – I was sure she wouldn't miss one.

I just about caught my train and met up with a friend called Cat. She was heading to see family in Liverpool and we spent the morning catching up together. As we were walking back through the park to catch our respective trains, I remembered the stone and peg in my pocket. I fumbled around, took them out and showed them to Cat.

'Take your pick,' I said.

She nervously took the peg with a look of 'what's the catch?'

'I dare you to use this peg to let someone know how God feels about them,' I said.

Cat is a good laugh and she took the dare. Smiling, she said, 'I presume you are going to do the same,' nodding at the pumice stone.

I like a challenge, so we shook hands – game on.

As we hurried on, we went past some workmen moving flagstones on the pathway. I toyed with the stone in my hand and looked at Cat for assurance. Cat smiled and laughed – she knew what was next.

I thought about it. In my mind, I couldn't really make any link between God and this silly pumice stone, never mind the disgruntled-looking workmen in front of me. The more I tried, the less sense it made. But then there was Cat, looking and laughing at me because it was me who had started this silly business.

I decided to stop thinking and took a deep breath – I went up to one of the men and handed him the stone. He took it and examined it silently. I didn't know what to say, so I simply told him it was a reminder of God's love for him and that God was his father.

He looked up and smiled at me. The scary workman became a human being.

'My son collects stones,' he said. 'Can I give it to him?'

'Course you can,' I nodded, as if that was the very intention behind my action.

Relaxing now, I told him that my daughter, too, collected stones. We chatted about our kids, the stones they had collected and where they had found them. I suggested that the way we feel about our kids is the same way that God feels about us – it made sense to both of us. It was bliss and funny, real and random – two dads, two kids, one father. I looked over at Cat, whose look said it all: 'You are soooo lucky.' We finished our conversation and I left the workman with the pumice stone for his son. My sense of joy was nearly matched by the smugness with which I swaggered over to Cat and reminded her about the peg in her pocket.

That evening, somewhere in Liverpool, somebody returned home and found that they had been pegged by a stranger. On that peg read the words: 'God loves you.'

Madeleine Delbrêl worked among the communists in some of the poorest parts of Paris in the years leading up to the Second World War. She is an example for me in her simple devotion to Jesus and the courage with which she lived out her convictions. She suggests that the extent of the kingdom of heaven in our lives can be seen in the small habits and decisions we make every day. Changing our habits is something we do all the time: wake up earlier, eat more healthily, drink less and so on – all habits that we adjust daily by making small decisions based on intention. Small intentions like carrying an object with you each day as a gift to offer someone, deciding to pay for a stranger's coffee, or leaving a prayer on the bus are small intentions that change people's lives. They are like small rips in the grey fabric of society through which the Light pierces and the kingdom of God is glimpsed.

Each day I take three objects out with me: my phone, my keys and my wallet. When I forget one of these, it soon becomes apparent and I become unable to function as planned that day. I can't get in the car, can't pay for my drink and then come home to a list of irate texts asking why I am not answering my phone. A while back, I decided that I would add an extra essential object to my list. Packing a little wooden cross, a battered metal heart or a pocket Bible would be part of my new daily routine and, if the occasion arose, I would give it away.

So that's what I do. As a result of this little habit, hundreds of people in shops, parks, hospitals and trains have been reminded of God's love for them. I have also noticed that when a group of friends, colleagues or a church develop this simple habit, the hundreds become thousands, and the extent of the kingdom of God spreads like a virus in our society. Developing a culture of challenge, fun and simplicity will bring life back to the routine of any group of people. St David, the Welsh Celtic saint, is reported to have said in some of his last words to his monks: 'Do the little things, the small things that you have heard and seen me do.' Somebody else once said that if you are not planning to do something, you are planning not to do it, and there is truth in this. So why not try a little thing. Start small. Look at what you carry around each day and plan to take something extra with you: a small reminder or a gift for a friend or a stranger. God occasionally works through our grand designs to change people's lives, but He continually responds to our small steps. This is because they are rooted in something powerful. That something is called faith.

10

The Trial

The gospel is to be sung as a choral piece, albeit with solos.[27]

One of my favourite ways to be good news in everyday life is to literally do nothing! That is easier said than done. It defies our flesh to believe that God does not need us to scheme up a clever evangelistic idea or a polished set of questions that we pull out when we meet people, but the reality is that He doesn't. To remind myself of this in everyday life, I will often make a point of stopping somewhere and doing nothing – nothing except watching the world go by and being available to God and the surrounding people. As a one-off it's a piece of cake, but try practising it regularly. It's more difficult than you think, but well worth it.

---

[27] This is my paraphrase of Brad J Kallenburg, *Live to Tell* (Grand Rapids, MI: Brazos Press, 2002), p49, who states that 'the gospel is sung not as a solo but as a choral piece'.

There is something about a person who is available, something that makes them approachable to others, just as there is something about a person 'on a mission' that makes them worth avoiding. To stop and be still with the Lord[28] in the busy street, on the bus or in the park also has a dynamic about it that I find curious. The reason I say this is because, very often, by sitting and doing nothing, I end up in the most incredible discussions with people who come to talk to me.

I was sitting with a friend, doing this very thing, in the town where I live. It was early summer and we sat on a city-centre bench, leisurely watching the people go by. As we did, we said prayers of blessing for people who caught our attention, and listened to God. I was playing with some cards called the Jesus Deck, which depict scenes from Jesus' life. As we sat there, two girls, who definitely should have been in school, sat down on the bench next to us. They watched *us* as we watched people.

'What you doing?' one of them quizzed me, like a police officer.

'Erm, dunno, praying,' I replied, taken aback by her direct manner.

She stared at me, unfazed. This was a kid with attitude.

'What's that?' she continued.

'What's what?' I replied.

'That.' She nodded at the cards.

The attitude was oozing.

'Why?' I shot back.

---

[28] Psalm 46:10.

'Cos I'm asking,' she retorted without any hesitation.

It was like an attitude ping-pong match and she was clearly better at this game than me. Saying nothing, I turned the cards over one by one, and then asked her to pick a card. She stood up and chose a card and held it out to me. I turned it over. It was a picture of Jesus on trial with the Pharisees the night before His execution. She clearly had no idea what it was or what it referred to. The nature of choosing something for yourself implicates you, and she wanted to know what it meant, for her.

I told her the story. She asked me why they put Him on trial and about the accusations. I explained the inability of the Pharisees to find a reason to condemn Him apart from His apparent claim to be God. She listened, but appeared unmoved by the story. I then told her that God had a plan for her life and this was part of that plan.

She then said a curious thing: 'Did He get off?'

Again, she had caught me off guard and I scrambled for my words. 'What do you mean?'

'What happened to Him?' she pressed me.

As a card-carrying Christian, I had to hide my surprise at her question. How come a fourteen-year-old kid growing up in twenty-first century Britain didn't know *if He got off*!

I composed myself and looked around. I noticed an older man listening in eagerly to our conversation.

'So what happened?' she pursued.

It is not the most difficult question to answer as a Christian. Concepts like suffering, heaven and hell, other religions, aliens and creation come much higher up the theological scale for me, but something about this simple question made me pause.

I remember how people asked Jesus apparently straightforward questions, but His answers drew their real intentions out. I wondered what Jesus would say to this girl and paused to hear God.

I asked her if she really did not know the story and she told me frankly, 'No.'

I believed her.

I told her it was ultimately important for her to find out because it was linked to the story of her own life; so important that I was not going to tell her myself, and if she really wanted to know, she would need to go and find out for herself.

'So?' She grew impatient.

'I told you, if you really want to know, go and find out for yourself. I am not going to tell you.'

Apparently, she really did want to know. At once, she stood up and walked over to the older guy who had been listening in and, bold as brass, asked him, 'Do you know what happened to Jesus after the trial?'

The man, also a little taken aback, replied, 'Yes.'

'Then tell me,' she demanded.

We listened as the man described the beating and whipping that Jesus had received. As my friend and I stood up and walked away, we could hear that guy telling the rest of the story. I am guessing and hoping he told her of the crucifixion, the resurrection and Jesus' offer of life to all who believe in and follow Him.

I was not the evangelist that day, but I was there, and evangelism happened.

Some of you might find my approach questionable, and you might be right. The truth is that I don't have all the answers and I often don't know *what* to say. The story goes that, one day, a lady criticised the great preacher D L Moody for his methods of evangelism. Moody conceded, 'I agree with you, I don't like the way I do it either. Tell me, how do you do it?' The lady replied, 'I don't do it.' To which Moody replied, 'Then I like my way of doing it better than your way of not doing it.'[29] We are all afraid of getting it wrong or messing it up, but I believe God honours a willingness to go and try.

This said, it *does* puzzle me how we live in the twenty-first century in a country with more than 1,000 years of faith behind it, when a young girl asks the question, 'Did He get off?' I am not annoyed with the girl, why should she know? I am uncomfortable with myself and the Church I am part of: shouldn't we be letting her, and millions of others like her, know? This is the story of her life and she doesn't even know it? But that uneasy truth sits heavily with most Christians and can lead to an unhelpful sense of guilt. In reaction, we sometimes excuse the fact that we are uncomfortable to share the story by leaving it to specialist evangelists. But in doing so, I think we lose a part of who we are as a Church. We are *all* the people of God, *all* the 'royal priesthood'[30] and *all* given a little piece of the jigsaw. When we delegate that to

---

[29] Paraphrased from a post on Theological Matters, https://theologicalmatters.com/2013/01/23/i-question-your-evangelism/ (accessed 26th November 2018).
[30] 1 Peter 2:9.

specialists, the picture of Jesus in the twenty-first century becomes patchy and obscure in ordinary life. That is why God has given us a truly wondrous gift – each other.

One December evening, a good friend and I had planned to dress up as an angel and a shepherd and go around the pubs in our town at Christmas, reminding people of the announcement of Jesus' arrival. We had our gowns on and our towels on our heads but, as we set out, my friend hesitated. He is one of the most courageous evangelists I know and well known locally and nationally for his daring escapades. But this evening, he faltered. He suggested that we stay in and pray about the people in the pub instead of actually going out to meet them. As you will read in my other stories, it is often *me* who falters, but this evening it was my friend. I had also wanted to stay at home that night, but the fact that I had come out into town and found myself dressed like my daughter in the nativity play was enough to threaten him with mild violence if he refused to get out of the door. He was convinced. We headed off like lambs to the slaughter. We didn't get far. In fact, we spent the whole evening chatting to the first guy we met in a pub about why God had come. It was worth it. Without each other, neither of us would have gone out that night and that man may never have had the opportunity to pose his questions, albeit with two weirdos dressed as an angel and a shepherd!

And that is the gift – togetherness. God sent out His friends *together* and they brought good news *together*. They relied on each other, and when one lacked, the other took up the slack. I remind the teams with whom I work that every time someone brings back a wonderful story, it belongs to all of them. Every time someone gets it wrong or messes it up, it is borne by all of them. Consequently, there are no superstars, just friends egging each other on.

Brad Kallenburg in his book, *Live to Tell*, argues that the gospel is to be sung as a choral piece, albeit with solos.[31] By this he means that the good news is best understood by people when it is presented by the whole body of the Church, warts and all, rather than just a special few. Clearly, we prize the role of gifted evangelists who deliver the message, often in large gatherings to many people, but these are the solos, and they must find their place in the symphony that involves us all. That means ordinary people like *you* and *me*. It rings true with Paul's letters referring to the body of Christ being made up of many parts and all parts having their unique vital function.[32]

My role, dressed as a shepherd, was to be the foolhardy one that night. My role, sat on the bench in the city centre, was to respond to the question from the girl with attitude, listen to God and then pass on the baton. Some of you will be thinking, as I often do, but what if that man told the story badly or he didn't stress the important bits? What if he wasn't a Christian? These are all good questions. However, God is sovereign, and we must trust Him. He is able to conduct His symphony very capably with those who trust and make themselves available to Him. Sometimes that means just playing *your* part, albeit a minor role.

---

[31] See footnote 27.

[32] See 1 Corinthians 12 and Romans 12.

Too many of us are bound by the idea that evangelism is a one-stop affair. This has led to a misunderstanding that each deal must be sealed by us personally, and herein lies the paradox. There is a very real urgency today when a fourteen-year-old doesn't know the story of Jesus, and so the need is great. However, shouldering that burden is too great for one person alone. It either crushes us through guilt into inertia, or causes us to act out of desperation, which is ultimately a recipe for autonomy. This is not the way in Scripture of Jesus and His followers, or the story that unfolds in the early Church. The bringing of good news is most definitely, and will always remain, a family affair, rooted in a dependence on each other and God.

11

Tigger

*Our churches ... They are holy places where the Spirit blows –
but outside, there is a Holy Spirit who blows in all places.*[33]

I have a friend and she *is* Tigger. That's not her real name,
but when I met her, that's what she reminded me of. If
you have not read the children's book *Winnie the Pooh*,
then you will not know what I am talking about. So, to
save you the effort, Tigger is a tiger in the story who is
constantly eager, bouncing around and infused with
enthusiasm.

I had arranged to meet Tigger one afternoon. She was
on a work placement with me, doing city-centre
chaplaincy. As a city centre chaplain, I spent time visiting
shops, chatting to people and, when appropriate, offering
prayer, advice or direction to local churches or services.

[33] This is a rewording of a phrase used by Madeleine Delbrêl,
Nous Autres, Gens des Rue, p63. Translated and paraphrased by
Glyn Jones.

Tigger arrived with her usual jubilation and gusto, enthusiastic to go and do some crazy stunt for Jesus. She was expecting some pretty mega things to happen that day. I, on the other hand, was not.

I was not feeling bouncy. In fact, I was feeling rather unenthusiastic and Tigger's zeal just made me feel even more deflated. If you *have* read *Winnie the Pooh*, then I was feeling more like Eeyore the donkey. That day, I wanted evangelism to be prayer or, more accurately, sleep. However, Tigger was there, 200 per cent, and so we headed off. She started to tell me how excited she was and machine-gunned me with questions: where were we going, who would we meet, what would happen, what was the plan? I felt my stomach churn – there was no plan, no destination, no one to meet and nothing would happen. Despite my mood, I decided it was only fair to Tigger that we go, and so we headed off.

As we walked, I tried to bring her expectations down to earth and explained that we were simply going for a walk and that evangelism sometimes meant a willingness to go, without encounter or expectation.

We strolled along together, with Tigger bobbing up and down like a float in the water. I listened to her wittering away and she brought a smile to my sullen face as we walked. Continuing along the canal towpath, I started to feel peckish. I suggested that we stop off at the shop – and we could ask at a moored canal boat whether they wanted anything from the shop while we were there. Tigger stopped in her tracks, smiled, and nodded knowingly. She looked at me as if I had just invented a cure for stupidity.

'Right,' she said, expectantly. 'This is it.' She had a certain knowing look in her eyes.

'We are just going to the shop,' I soberly reminded her.

We approached the moored narrowboat and looked to see if there was anyone around. Hearing someone talking quietly inside, we drew alongside the open window and paused.

It was an odd thing, to hear familiar words being read in an unfamiliar way – slowly, and with painful hesitation: 'I am Alpha and Omega, the beginning and the ending, saith the Lord …'[34]

A lady sat reading in deep concentration, pausing between words and putting emphasis on unusual syllables, as if she was unable to get it right – she was clearly not used to reading this.

We listened, fascinated, and looked on. She sat with her bare feet up on the sofa, wearing a knitted eco-warrior-style cardigan. Grasping a small, worn, leather Bible, she pored over the words as if trying to decipher an ancient manuscript.

The lady continued, 'which is, and which was, and which is to come.'[35]

Sensing the presence of people outside her boat, she looked up. She didn't say anything to us, but just gazed in a slightly pained and distracted way. She inspected Tigger and then her gaze fell on me.

'Erm, hello,' I stuttered.

She nodded at me. Tigger edged forward as if to pounce.

---

[34] Revelation 1:8, KJV.

[35] Revelation 1:8, KJV.

'We were just going to the shop, and ... erm ...' I paused. 'What are you reading?' I asked, revealing my true question.

'This.' She held out the book to us and I saw the title, 'The King James Bible'. 'Someone gave me this Bible and I can't make any sense of it.'

Tigger edged further forward.

'It talks about the Alpha and the Omega. Do you have *any* idea what it is talking about?' she enquired, genuinely expecting two complete strangers outside her canal boat to know.

'Jesus!' someone shrieked involuntarily. I can only imagine it was my friend, Tigger.

The woman looked up, puzzled. 'Oh,' she said, slowly manoeuvring herself off the couch and making her way to the back entrance of the boat with her little book.

As she emerged, she leaned, as if to relieve pain, on the boat's tiller. We now saw a slightly stout lady with a kindly face. Her greying hair was tied up. Her ruddy features gave the impression of someone who spent a long time in the fresh air and was used to not having to look tidy for others.

She just looked at us and said nothing.

I explained that we were going to the shop and had wondered if she needed anything. She thanked us for the offer, but said she had all she needed.

'Why are you reading the Bible?' I asked.

She told us that someone had given her the book a while ago and she read it whenever she felt anxious, but often she found the meaning obscure. She went on to tell us briefly about her difficulties with reading, and the anxiety that waxed and waned in her life.

My friend was amazing and, despite being Tigger, she listened carefully to every word, acknowledging the difficulties that the lady faced. She didn't interrupt her once and nodded – albeit eagerly – all the way through.

We spent a brief amount of time with this lady and told her about Jesus, who had changed our lives and gave us peace in our anxious moments. We explained what we understood about the Alpha and the Omega: Jesus who holds everything and who offers to hold us. We prayed with her and offered to drop another copy of the Bible back with her, one in more everyday language. I pledged to underline all the things the Bible said about peace. She seemed to find that helpful and so we parted ways.

As we strolled off, Tigger just looked at me, nodding, smiling, and still bobbing up and down. 'You were right all along. Isn't God great?' she exclaimed. 'We just need to go in faith, and amazing things happen without us even looking for them.'

Her faith was through the roof, only to be matched by my shame.

I coughed and murmured some lame agreement, too embarrassed to admit how reluctant I had been as I had set out that day.

As we made our way back that day, nothing would have surprised me. Had we met an Ethiopian eunuch in a chariot discussing the book of Isaiah with Philip the evangelist, I wouldn't have batted an eyelid.[36]

---

[36] If you have no idea what I am referring to, read Acts 8!

Part of my role is to visit churches and help them think about how they can relate Christianity to people around them. I ask them lots of questions and look at who they are and the people they are trying to connect with. One of the most common things I hear when visiting new churches is the phrase 'we are a welcoming church'. In fact, if I had £1 for every time I heard 'we are a welcoming church', I would be a very rich man. However, what does it mean to be a welcoming church?

Have you ever arrived at a social event and realised you don't know anyone? You walk into a strange room and see people chatting and socialising. They all appear to know each other, but *you* don't seem to know anyone. You scan the room in the hope of seeing a familiar face – but you don't. You feel isolated, awkward, alone, and most of us would quickly pull out a smartphone, head for the drinks, or sometimes just leave. Several of my good friends will avoid these occasions at all costs and make an excuse not to go.

What we really need in this situation is someone to come over and say hello. Somebody to see us, to leave their happy huddle, cross the room, and welcome us in. This is the true meaning of welcome and inclusion. Not just to open the door, but to go out and invite. This is also the true meaning of biblical mission. To say we are 'welcoming' or 'inclusive' without being willing to go, leave our services and buildings and cross the neighbourhood to say hello and invite people to join us is a hollow claim.

The reason this seems so unfamiliar to many of us is that for years, decades and centuries, our churches and communities were so intertwined with the fabric of one another that we didn't need to go out and invite. People came into church as they would come into a pub or a shop. That is no longer the case. And so we must recapture the nature of welcome: to go and to invite. In our dis-ease with true welcome, we focus on improving the music, the coffee, the lights and the tech, none of which requires us to set foot outside the building. Don't get me wrong, none of these things are bad things in themselves, but if a child walked among us, they might state the obvious – we don't want to go out and invite people in.

I believe our churches and gatherings are for the most part wonderful places, full of great people and good news. They are holy places where the Spirit blows – but outside, there is a Holy Spirit who blows in all places.[37] This means if we truly want to be places of welcome, we will need to become a people 'born of the Spirit'[38] and willing to go and be sent.

The word 'mission', translated from the New Testament Greek, means 'sent', sent by God. It is the word used in the passage when the master of the house sends out the servants:

> So the servants went out into the streets and gathered all the people they could find, the bad

---

[37] See footnote 33.
[38] John 3.8.

as well as the good, and the wedding hall was filled with guests.[39]

Jesus had an uncanny knack of sending people out wherever they were, inadequacies and all, to invite people in. The story of the wedding banquet in Matthew 22 paints this picture wonderfully, and so to follow Him, we must be a people who recapture the meanings of 'go' and 'welcome'. In the words of the Baptist missionary Hudson Taylor: 'The Great Commission is not an option to be considered; it is a command to be obeyed.'[40]

However, it is not only a command, but more importantly, it is also our identity. We are children of God, made of the same spiritual stuff as Jesus, the man who was willing to go and invite people to join Him. As such, whenever we lose this capacity of true welcome, a part of us shrivels up and dies, as individuals and as churches.

To recapture this means having the courage to learn again who we truly are and the nature of our missional DNA. We are the people who welcome, the people who go out and invite others to come back. It will be new or strange for many of us at first, but like muscles and movements that have not been used for years, the pain and stiffness will ease with gentle flexing and stretching, and what seemed unnatural will become strong and

---

[39] Matthew 22:10.

[40] Quote by Hudson Taylor, https://www.goodreads.com/quotes/799214-the-great-commission-is-not-an-option-to-be-considered (accessed 3rd December 2018).

supple. We will realise that this is how we were designed to function; each of us do this in a different way. Some of us will be spontaneous, some organised; some will go in groups, and others on their own – there is no 'one size fits all'. Some days you will feel like Eeyore the donkey, but press on, it's worth it. The result will be the same: an invitation to a banquet.

12

The Rubbish Doll

Have a word with yourself about who God is, then let Him be that. Then have a word with God about who you are, then let yourself be that.

'It's a disgrace,' a lady said, as she walked past me.

I nodded in agreement, giving her an 'I know, but what can you do?' shrug.

She paused, shook her head, and carried on complaining to a young child she had in tow.

I stood there.

'What on earth do we pay the council for?' another person muttered, hurrying past on their way back to work.

I did my dumb look, again.

I was stood in a busy pedestrian area of a city centre. Next to me, strewn across the cobbles, were crisp bags, nappies, empty bottles, chip bag wrappers and all kinds of nasty-smelling rubbish. Passers-by looked on with horror and made comments to reassure me that they too found it an utter disgrace.

A more attentive onlooker may have noticed that this was not, however, a haphazard pile of random rubbish left by the council workers. A carefully laid rope surrounded the rubbish, marking its boundary, and in the centre there was a space, with a baby doll in a wooden crib. The council rubbish collectors had, in fact, taken quite some convincing to let me empty out my numerous bags of rubbish in the middle of their immaculately swept street. I had had to beg and barter, vowing to clear it up afterwards. They had reluctantly consented, but just for a short time. (I had actually told them I was with the local church, which was true, but had been careful not to specify which church.)

Two girls approached, one pushing a pram. They jabbered enthusiastically, interrupting, agreeing, laughing and nodding at one other, completely consumed in their conversation and unaware of the scene unfolding around them. They stopped abruptly, in front of the rubbish, and stared. Neither one said a word.

One girl frowned. It was as if she was trying to compute what it was.

She looked at me.

'What is it?' she said, as if I were a museum curator next to a piece of contemporary art.

'It's a story,' I said.

'It's a story alright,' she declared. She nudged her friend and they fell about in laughter.

'What's the story about?' she asked, composing herself.

'You need to work it out,' I replied. 'What do you see?'

'A load of rubbish,' she shot back. 'Is it about the environment, climate change, the messed-up planet?' She machine-gunned ideas at me.

'Yes,' I said. 'It is about a messed-up world, spot on.'

'It's terrible, isn't it,' her friend piped up in agreement. 'Someone should do something about it before it's too late.'

'That's the story,' I said. 'It's about a man who did something about it.'

'Who was it?' they both asked in unison.

'You need to work it out,' I said, regretfully. 'What happens when people make a stand against something that is wrong?'

'They probably put him away or even killed him. Was it Martin Luther King?' asked one of them.

'No. Good try, though,' I encouraged her.

'Gandhi?' she tried again.

'No.' My head nodded slightly to let her know she was nearly there. 'Would you follow someone who had the guts to stand up and be counted, so much so that He was willing to die for it?'

They pondered the question.

'Yes,' replied the louder girl who had started the conversation.

'Yeah,' agreed her friend. 'So who was He?'

'He's in the middle of the story.' I motioned towards the baby doll in the crib at the centre of the rubbish.

They looked at the scene, pondered, and then the penny dropped.

I explained the story of Jesus, who came to a world that had become polluted and filled with foul-smelling stuff. And He stood up and said it was wrong and announced another way to live. And for doing so, they killed Him. But death couldn't beat Him, and He rose again, and offers to all the opportunity to follow Him and become people who make a stand against the wrong of this world.

They listened as I retold the story back to them.

I concluded, 'So, would *you* follow Him?'

They pondered the question for a second.

'Oh, we're Catholic,' one suddenly blurted out, as if to reassure herself.

'Brilliant,' I replied. 'What does that involve?'

They told me about growing up in school and about going to church as kids, but as they spoke, they weren't certain what that meant for them now as adults. We chatted a bit more about what following Jesus meant. About the challenge of not just trying to be a good person, but the toughest challenge of all: to give up on self and others and wholly rely on God – the paradox of grace. I left them with a dare to renew their faith in Jesus and follow the doll in the rubbish.

The difficult truth of the matter is that the gospel will always involve an element of challenge. It is ultimately not a call to try harder, do better, speak more nicely and be a better Catholic, Protestant or whatever – no, it is ultimately a call to die. As such, it requires everything: to die to everything and to rise into a new life, one in relationship with God and all people through Him in a new way. That can be a tough call, especially when it involves our everyday friendships and people we care about deeply: those who depend upon us and on whom we depend. And so it can be a delicate and sensitive thing to bring this challenge to the people we care for most. It is one thing having a conversation in the street with a stranger, but it is entirely another to pose the ultimate challenge to a lifelong friend or family member. Ironically, those we care about most may never get a chance to respond to that challenge unless we both embody God's grace and offer it to them.

And this is the pitfall for many of us. Embodying and presenting such a monumental claim requires a degree of credibility, something that many of us feel we lack as Christians. We don't feel good enough to make God's claim, because our own lives are patchy at best. And so this leads to a cycle of grief: try harder, do better, be a perfect Christian – something that most of us fail at, spectacularly and daily. However, we need to remember something very important about the good news of Jesus Christ: it does not belong to us and does not depend on us; it is not *our* good news. Consequently, we are not required to justify it or apologise for it; it is what it is – a call to die and a call to live.

I must admit, I don't go for many formulas as an evangelist, but this is one that helps me daily with this issue: let God be God, you be yourself, and if anyone's interested, tell them.[41] It stems from the fisherman Peter in the Bible:

---

[41] This was inspired by Danielle Strickland's teaching at the New Wine leaders' conference in Harrogate, 2016.

But in your hearts revere Christ as Lord. Always be prepared to give an answer to everyone who asks you to give the reason for the hope that you have. But do this with gentleness and respect.[42]

It means thinking about who God really is and then not taking responsibility for Him: He is who He is.[43] It then means taking seriously your own identity in Christ, as a child who is loved, cherished, accepted and trusted by God. The living out of your true identity is a whole load simpler than the living up to everyone else's expectations, and far less punishing. And in doing so, you don't need to crowbar God into your life and your conversations; He forms a natural part of them. As do your family, friends, job, football team, hobbies, and so on.

Despite its simplicity, I do find this simple formula remarkably evasive at times. I find myself giving God a helping hand and trying to make Him something He is not. Allowing God to be God and His claims in Jesus to stand for themselves can be liberating: they are not *our* claims, they are His.

At other times, I find myself exaggerating my *own* achievements or even failures, frightened that the real me is lacking in some way. Both these pitfalls lack integrity and authenticity, and people will read that and project it onto God. But when we manage to let God be God and ourselves be ourselves, faith rings true without it being contrived or awkward. It also allows the challenge of the

[42] 1 Peter 3:15.
[43] Exodus 3:13-14.

gospel to be posed with integrity and stand on its own terms. So, try it out: have a word with yourself about who God is, then let Him be that. Then have a word with God about who *you* are, then let yourself be that. If anyone is interested, let them know, and try not to be an idiot about it!

Postscript

Our lives are a patchwork of stories: good stories, sad stories, bad stories, embarrassing and inspiring stories. We all have our own stories to tell. I come from a family that is used to telling its stories and I have felt the profound effect of their power in my life. I am a follower of Jesus today because of those stories told to me: from family, friends, at church and in the Bible. When I read the Bible, I am blown away by the stories of Jesus and the heroes of the faith. But I am also captivated by the stories of the ordinary people in whose lives God weaves hope and change. My prayer is that you feel encouraged to try some of the ideas in this book out for yourself and, in doing so, to make your own stories with God. Then tell those stories. Tell them to your family, your friends, at work, in the pub and in church. And people will come to know for themselves that there really is a God, and that God is good.